The Moose

Gentle Giant

text by Christian Havard
photos by Michel Blachas and Carole Piché

i꩜i Charlesbridge

Library of Congress Cataloging-in-Publication Data
Havard, Christian.
      [Elan. English]
   The moose: gentle giant / Christian Havard; photographs by
Michel Blachas and Carole Piché; [translation by Lisa Laird].
      p.   cm.—(Animal close-ups)
   Includes bibliographical references (p. 28).
   Summary: Text and photographs describe the appearance,
behavior, breeding, and habitat of the moose.
      ISBN 1-57091-505-9 (softcover)
      1. Moose—Juvenile literature. [1. Moose.] I. Blachas, Michel ill.
II. Piché, Carole ill. III. Title. IV. Series.
QL737.U55 H37513 2002
599.65'7—dc21   2001004365

Copyright © 1998 by Éditions Milan under the title *l'elan, roi couronné*
300 rue Léon-Joulin, 31101 Toulouse Cedex 100, France
French series editor, Valérie Tracqui

Published by Charlesbridge Publishing, 85 Main Street, Watertown, MA 02472
(617) 926-0329 • www.charlesbridge.com

Moose are found in the northern parts of North America, Europe, and Asia.

A solitary life

On a fall morning, the forest is dressed in brilliant colors—red maple, yellow aspen, and orange willow. Snow geese rest on a lake before continuing their long flight south. Bit by bit, nature wakes, warmed by the first rays of the sun.

At the edge of the forest, leaves rustle. A pack of wolves is returning to its den after a long night's hunt. The wolves run swiftly, thinking only of sleep.

Their passing does not disturb the majestic giant that approaches the lake. It is a moose, the biggest deer in the world. Walking clumsily, the big moose slips into the icy water and begins to eat.

An odd animal

The moose has the long legs of a giraffe, the body of a horse, and the nose of a camel. A crown of antlers rests high on the male's head. A moose's neck is short and a flap of skin and hair, called the bell, hangs from its throat. When it walks with its head down, a moose looks like it has a hump on its back.

A moose can grow up to seven and a half feet tall at the shoulder and weigh up to 1,800 pounds. Nevertheless, it can move through the forest without making a sound. Brown-black fur helps the giant disappear in the shadow of the trees if a predator is near.

Moose cannot see very well, but they have excellent hearing and a strong sense of smell.

Only the male moose, called a bull, grows antlers. Some antlers spread more than six feet wide and weigh up to forty-five pounds.

Wide, divided hooves help moose walk comfortably on marshy ground. Even so, moose are so heavy that they sometimes get stuck in the mud.

Although moose do not mark their territory with their droppings as other animals do, moose pellets are a natural fertilizer. They also provide food for some insects.

The female moose, or cow, can hardly reach the water because her neck is so short. The cow has to drop to her knees or spread her front legs wide to drink. This position is dangerous because it makes her vulnerable to predators.

Moose's hearts beat faster when their body temperatures rise above fifty degrees Fahrenheit.
In hot weather, moose often take baths to cool down.

To keep water from getting in their noses, moose take a deep breath and then close their nostrils. Moose can hold their breath for over one minute.

A watery meal

Moose do not have distinct territories. Two moose may share the shores of lakes. They ignore each other and focus on the water lilies and other aquatic plants they love to eat.

Moose dunk their heads underwater to gently pull out the plants with their teeth. Occasionally, moose swim or dive as deep as sixteen feet.

Moose eat up to forty-five pounds of plants per day. In the fall, they eat even more to build up body fat that will help keep them warm in the winter. Moose do not migrate, but they may swim up to twelve miles to find a quiet place with good food.

This moose shakes his antlers to chase away pesky mosquitoes, but sometimes diving is the only way to escape the parasites that cling to him.

Mating season

Bull moose are usually peaceful animals, but they become aggressive during mating season. They paw the earth with their hooves, urinate, and then roll in the puddle to make their coat smell as strongly as possible. Then bulls rub against trees to make others aware of their presence in this part of the forest.

Attracted by these signals, a cow moans loudly. Several bulls may respond to her call, but she allows only one to mate. The bulls charge each other. Their antlers lock in the struggle to prove which bull is strongest. One of the bulls loses his footing and is forced to his knees—he has lost. The loser disappears into the trees.

Bulls are able to reproduce when they are two years old, but have little chance of winning a fight until they are at least five.

The winner follows the cow by her smell, which tells him she is ready to mate. Afterwards, the bull looks for other cows to mate with.

A terrible hunger

In winter, moose leave frozen lakes and marshes to take refuge in the forest. Cows usually live alone, but now they gather in small groups with a few young males. It is hard to find food. Together, moose scrape at the snow to turn up tufts of grass.

Moose huddle to help keep warm during the cold winter. This group is lucky to find a fallen tree with many small branches to eat.

When mating season is over, bulls' antlers fall out, usually between November and February, depending on the moose's age. Sometimes a bull loses one antler before the other, which can throw him off balance. Until summer, a bull's only weapons are his hooves.

Long legs let moose walk easily through a foot and a half of snow.

As winter goes on and other food cannot be found, moose eat twigs, bark, and lichen. Caribou graze along the ground, but moose often look for food higher up. Balancing on their back legs, they rest their front legs on a tree trunk to reach high branches. Moose constantly search for more food to stay alive. Many die from hunger or become too weak to outrun bears or wolves.

In winter, moose eat a few mouthfuls of snow to get water. There may be food under the snow they eat.

Moose lose about half their weight during winter. In spring they feast on water plants, buds, and new leaves to regain strength.

Patch by patch, thick winter fur falls out. Thin, molting moose look very ragged in the spring.

A moose's trimming during the winter may help trees sprout in the spring.

Spring is here

Hard winter is over—the strongest animals survived. In the soft spring afternoon, the first buds burst open. The small group of moose has separated, as each animal returns to its solitary life. Yearling moose leave their mothers, but do not go far—just far enough to prove that they know how to take care of themselves.

Big bulls feel the first growth of new antlers. Babies grow in cows' bellies. About eight months after mating, cows look for quiet places to give birth. They may swim to an island, but more often cows find a small, grassy clearing in the woods with water nearby.

Summer fur is shorter and cooler for the hot weather. The individual hairs are hollow, which act as an insulator to keep the moose warm.

15

A beautiful baby

The baby moose, called a calf, can weigh up to thirty-five pounds at birth and stand up to two and a half feet tall. Unlike many baby deer, newborn moose fur does not have white spots. Instead, it is a beautiful caramel color.

Calves soon try to stand. Despite long, shaky legs, they manage a step or two before collapsing in the grass. Cows do not try to help, but they do lick their calves all over to hide the newborns' smell from passing predators.

Before long, calves become hungry. They awkwardly nuzzle their mothers' sides as they look for milk. After the calves drink their fill, they sleep hidden in thick bushes.

In the first days after birth, a calf is often left alone. It waits patiently, without moving.

Danger!

Calves grow quickly, doubling in weight in their first three weeks. They drink mother's milk five or six times a day, and also begin to eat a few poplar and hazel leaves.

Baby moose are very energetic. They play near their mothers, who never let them out of sight. Cows must be watchful—wolves howl nearby! Wolves sometimes hunt moose calves.

Bears are terrifying enemies for moose, young or old.

As soon as they are big enough, young moose follow their mothers as they look for food. Cows are the babies' only protection against predators.

18

As cows age, their chances of giving birth to twins or even triplets increase.
A mother must defend all her young with her powerful hooves.

Wolves tend to attack injured or older moose. This natural selection helps
keep the population strong.

Cows will stand their ground to defend their babies. Wolves may try to separate them, but they know a cow's kicks can be deadly. Sometimes the wolves win anyway.

A cow decides to cross a river, but the rushing water may frighten her calf. Nevertheless, the calf follows its mother. Mother and calf reach the other side and take a well-deserved rest.

Life goes on

The first year of life is hard for a baby moose. It must survive hunger, accidents, disease, and attacks from predators and hunters. Only half of the calves born each year reach adulthood. When fall arrives, calves stop drinking mother's milk and grow their first winter coat to keep warm during storms.

A male's antlers grow half an inch each day. Only small bumps show on a five-month-old's head.

A thick, soft skin, full of blood vessels, called velvet, covers the moose's antlers. When the antlers have reached their full height for the year, the velvet dies and drops away in strips.

The antlers of a two- or three-year-old look like short spikes.

A four- or five-year-old's antlers begin to branch out and have a distinctive paddle shape.

With their velvet removed, the antlers look very white. Moose rub their antlers against trees, which gives them their distinctive brown color. Antlers also darken with age.

A two-year-old carries his first set of antlers. They will not develop branches for another year. New branches grow every year along with the old ones. The wide paddles appear when a moose is five years old.

After the velvet wears off at the end of the summer, bulls are ready to fight for a mate.

By the time a bull is seven or eight, his antlers are fully developed.

The call of the wild

As the months pass, young moose learn to live alone in the forest. They find lakes filled with plants, berries, and twigs. They know how to escape from wolves and bears.

A year-old calf is not yet independent. Its mother has been its only teacher. Its father does not stay with the cow and her young.

As fall arrives, bulls' bellows echo through the forest. Their awesome antlers are ready for fighting. They huff and puff threateningly. Mating season is starting again, and big bulls hope to mate with the cows to continue the cycle of life in the forest.

The following fall, cows begin to moan for mates. The year-old calves stay with their mothers during the winter before striking out on their own in the spring.

A delicate balance

Moose arrived in North America about one million years ago, but nearly disappeared by the end of the nineteenth century. The giant animal was hunted close to extinction, and only thanks to strong conservation laws does it still roam the northern forests. Hunters still kill many moose, and new roads and mines continue to destroy their territory.

As people occupy more areas of moose habitat, overgrazing can become a problem.

Trophy hunting

Hunting moose is still legal throughout the animal's habitat. It has been a long time since Native Americans hunted them with bows and arrows, killing only as many as they needed to survive. Today's sport hunters kill animals for their heads, which they hang like trophies in their homes. Fortunately, many moose have learned to hide from these hunters.

Too big an appetite?

Studies have shown that moose sometimes destroy too much of their forest home by eating too many plant buds, which may prevent new growth in the forest.

Other scientists disagree. They think the way moose prune trees might help the trees to bud in the spring. It is hard to know which theory is right, so people often plant mixed forests to help preserve the natural balance among different kinds of trees.

Moose crave salt. After roads
have been salted to melt the snow and ice,
moose often lick them. Unfortunately, this
can cause terrible car accidents.

Taming the moose

In northern Europe, people have tried to tame moose. The animals' powerful muscles and gentle-seeming behavior make them appear perfect for harnessing and hauling heavy loads. However, moose are also stubborn and quick-tempered, so they can be hard to train. During mating season, bulls are unpredictable and dangerous.

Moose crossing

Many moose are hit by cars each year, especially during mating season, when males may charge anything that moves and often race across roadways in their excitement. Because of their great size, moose often cause a great deal of damage to cars, but in the end, moose usually come out the worst. If cars do not kill moose on impact, wolves or bears are likely to catch them before their injuries heal.

Moose are often seen crossing roads in populated areas. However, people should never approach a moose. Though they may seem tame, moose are wild animals and may attack if they feel provoked.

25

Moose cousins

Moose are part of the Cervid family, along with forty-one other species around the world. These peaceful animals vary in size from the smallest, the tiny pudu that stands fifteen inches tall at the shoulder, up to the largest, the moose. All cervids are even-toed, hoofed mammals, and most have antlers that drop off each year and grow back in a few months. Only the Chinese water deer lacks antlers.

▲ *Wapiti*, or *elk*, is a subspecies of the red deer that lives in Canada and the United States. They are much bigger than the European red deer, standing five feet tall at the shoulder. Wapiti eat only grass and berries, so they may share territory with moose. During mating season, male wapiti gather harems of females.

◀ *North American caribou* are called reindeer in Europe and Asia. Unlike other deer, both male and female caribou have antlers. Many children recognize caribou as the animals that pull Santa Claus's sleigh on Christmas Eve. During spring and fall, caribou migrate across the arctic tundra in large herds.

◀ Originally from the Mediterranean region, *fallow deer* can now be found worldwide. Their tan coats, spotted with white, are perfect camouflage in the underbrush where they live. The paddle-shaped antlers look like miniature versions of moose antlers, but, unlike moose, which grow antlers on either sides of their heads, fallow deer antlers grow right on top.

Roe deer are perhaps the most common deer in Europe. They hide during the day and come out at night to feed on the high grass at the forest edge or on wheat and corn in farmers' fields. During mating season, males, called roebucks, aggressively pursue females. ▶

For Further Reading on Moose . . .

Dutemple, Lesley A. *Early Bird Nature Books: Moose*. Lerner Publishing Group, 1998.

Fredericks, Anthony D. *Moose: Our Wild World Series*. Creative Publishing International, 2000.

Hemstock, Annie. *The Moose: Wildlife of North America*. Capstone Press, 1999.

Hodge, Deborah. *Deer, Moose, Elk, & Caribou*. Kids Can Press, 1998.

To See Moose in Captivity . . .

Folzenlogen, Darcy and Robert. *The Guide to American Zoos and Aquariums*. Willow Press, 1993.

Nyhuis, Allen W. *The Zoo Book: A Guide to America's Best*. Carousel Press, 1994.

Many zoos also have Web sites on the Internet. To learn more about their exhibits, go to:
http://dir.yahoo.com/science/biology/zoology/zoos

Use the Internet to Find Out More about the Moose. . . .

Alaska Department of Fish and Game Wildlife Notebook Series
—Learn about the moose's life history, habits, habitat, predators, and other dangers, including the impact of human population. Turn to the ADF&G home page for a link that describes what to do if you meet an aggressive moose.
http://www.state.ak.us/adfg/notebook/biggame/moose.htm

Go Moose
—Hear a moose call; find out about the moose's scientific classification and what it means; get tips for viewing moose safely; and enter a moose photo contest!
http://www.gomoose.com/moosefacts.html

Kachemak Heritage Land Trust
—How can people coexist with moose? Learn how we affect the moose's daily life and habitat, and discover how we can help moose survive in wilderness areas.
http://www.xyz.net/~khltkbr/projects/moose/index.html

University of Michigan Museum of Zoology: Animal Diversity Web
—Discover the behavior and habits of the moose and find out where you are most likely to meet one.
http://animaldiversity.ummz.umich.edu/accounts/alces/a._alces

63,455

DATE DUE

Jun 19 09		
Jul 7 09		
Aug 26 0		
Aug 3 04		
MAY 1 3 2013		
JUN 2 6 2013		
NOV 2 8 2016		